FRANCE

THE FOUR SEASONS

FRANCE
THE FOUR SEASONS

Photographs *by* Michael Busselle   Commentary *by* Frederic Raphael

CROSS RIVER PRESS
A DIVISION OF ABBEVILLE PUBLISHING GROUP
NEW YORK   LONDON   PARIS

First published in the United States of America in 1994
by CROSS RIVER PRESS, a Division of Abbeville Publishing Group,
488 Madison Avenue, New York, NY 10022

First published in Great Britain in 1994 by
PAVILION BOOKS LIMITED
26 Upper Ground, London SE1 9PD

ISBN 1-55859-869-3

Illustrated on page one:
Early June sees poppies in full bloom filling a meadow
near the village of Ste-Anastasie in
the *département* of Gard.
Illustrated on page two:
A field of sunflowers in mid-July faces the early-morning
sunlight near the village of Brancion in the *département* of
Saône-et-Loire.
Illustrated on page three:
Spring foliage at the beginning of May in the
Forêt de Boulogne near the village of Mont-près-Chambord
in the *département* of Loir-et-Cher.

CONTENTS

INTRODUCTION

Tourism is, perhaps, the only modern form of innocence; leaving political attitudes at home, its soft invaders contrive to look on other countries and societies only as instances of landscape. When it comes to France, what the tourist sees is so varied and so apparently *natural* that he or she can scarcely be blamed for reading its countryside for an Arcadia. Cyril Connolly, for instance, pinched in the austerity of wartime London, remembered the 'Virgilian landscape' of the Dordogne with hungry nostalgia; in *The Unquiet Grave*, he drew a circle, with a radius of twenty miles, its centre in the medieval town of Sarlat, to indicate the paradise where he would choose to live when he could escape from what Byron called 'the tight little island'. It so happens that for the last twenty-three years we have spent a great deal of time, in every season, in just that region. What we may have lost in innocence we have re-invested in respect for the year-long effort required to make the landscape scan like poetry. When Albert Camus said, 'We must imagine Sisyphus *happy*,' he might have been thinking of the peasant and the interminable cycle of labours to which his mistress, the earth, obliges him, year after year. '*Heureux*' could be said to conceal '*heures*', the hours of punctual effort required to procure the appearance of happiness.

There are easier ways to make a living. The depopulation of paradise proves it. Our house was once several houses, sheltering three families and the animals whose heat, permeating from below, supplemented their own. Our hill-top *lieu-dit*, Lagardelle, was once a village, with some sixty *feux* – the Périgourdins count fires, not houses – and its own bakery, which is now our dilapidated, ivy-wigged boundary mark. Today, there are only three working fire-places: our own, our Dutch neighbours' and that of the Barats, who farm most of the land which falls away from our three-valleyed eminence. Its eponymous, twelfth-century guard-tower was built by the English when they lorded it in Aquitaine; the unsagging lines of mortarless stone, pink and grey, russet and ochre, are as steady as the Buffs. Traditions of anonymous art reach back, in our region, to Cro-Magnon man.

Some twenty millennia ago, his secret playfulness or arcane mysteries (no one quite knows the purpose of his vivid art) impelled him to fill the limestone recesses of Lascaux and a plethora of other ventriform caves with the mammoth images of rural fauna, perhaps in appeasement of the hunted animals, perhaps in the hope of procuring their capture by its proleptic enactment. Beauty, in the countryside, is rarely without some practical purpose; that *is* its beauty. (Country cookery is the art of using up scraps, of presenting cheap ingredients in aromatic combinations, of giving mutton the allure of lamb.)

The pretty vision of country life which critics call pastoral began in the Alexandria of the Ptolemies, whose literati avoided the rusticity they celebrated so artificially. Nor is it likely that Marie Antoinette, playing at milkmaidenly simplicities with her pampered ladies-in-waiting at the end of the eighteenth century, knew anything of the burdensome drudgery she mimicked so prettily. The peasant has long suffered not only from the unremitting demands of his land and his animals but also from the urbane notion that he lived an enviable life. He can be forgiven for regarding such idyllic imputations as the last straw.

'*L'homme fait la terre,*' Emile Zola observed in his magnificent and muddy novel, *La Terre*, which derides the Rousseauesque illusions that nobility is a function of a 'natural' life and that Mother Earth furnishes an easy breast to which man can always repair for bountiful recreation. If Jean-Jacques had done some field-work, during his long stays with indulgent *châtelains*, he would have received an unsentimental education in the realities of a social contract which kept pre-Revolutionary peasants in a state of subjection hardly to be distinguished from serfdom. In the Middle Ages, the clergy and the nobility could help themselves to their minions' offspring quite as if children were part of the livestock over which the servile classes had no parental right whatever. *Droit de seigneur* warranted the nobility to help themselves to a low-born bride's virginity with no more conscience than they felt when they hanged her father for the insolence of killing game in his own fields; however destructive it might be, or however hungry the peasant's family, it was criminal not to preserve it for the lordly hunt. How many of the tourists who still regard the peasant as part of the landscape know anything of the ancestral blood and sweat which have gone into it?

The charm of the French is as artful as that of the great cathedrals which spring from their plains to crown the towns whose bourgeoisie profited from the produce carted to its halls. If France is its own finest work of art, its beauty has been fought and slaved for; the relation of the peasant to the land is one of ardent, often disputed, possession. Pierre-Jakez Hélias, in *The Horse of Pride*, his first-hand account of life in a Breton village after the Great War, tells of a farmer's refusal to install an indoor privy, even though he could well afford it. Such a luxury would have deprived him of a greater one, that of going out into his fields and digging a hole, wherever he felt like it. His shit both enriched the land and asserted his mastery over it.

Ownership is not a matter of title deeds but of physical, almost of sexual domination. To Zola's archetypal Beauceron peasant, *le père* Fouan, his land was like a unageing woman whose furrow, once he became impotent, could not be denied to the next generation. The son did not succeed his father so much as supplant him. *Le père* Fouan's gesture of crumbling a clod of earth between the fingers is heavy with ambiguity; the earth can never be retained for long: it falls back into itself and no man possesses for ever what, in the end, always comes to possess him.

The department of the Beauce comprises the great plain which stretches down from south of Paris, past Chartres and Orléans as far as the forests of the Sologne. To the fast traveller it is a landscape without marked charm, like Spain's La Mancha, but Zola saw it as a hive of greed, intrigue and family feuds, while Marcel Proust – whose Combray was an imaginative gloss on the lustreless little town of Illiers – remembered it as vibrant with the hawthorn along the Guermantes Way, a breath-taking garden of hay-feverish delights. The secret country mansion – the great good place where true love might be found – haunted Alain-Fournier's romantic appetite. His hero in *Le Grand Meaulnes*, lost in the unmapped thickets of the Cher, near Blois, falls upon an enchanted household and is sweetly haunted by the vision of what becomes an irrecoverable passion. Town-houses have addresses; country houses are magically unnumbered.

Proust had none of Tolstoy's emulous sympathy with the peasant; one cannot imagine Marcel matching – or wanting to match – the reapers cut for cut, as

Levin did in *Anna Karenina*. *Le petit* Marcel had no nerve for the unsubtleties of country life: he was shocked by the curses which the family servant, Françoise, loaded on an uncooperative chicken which she was trying to decapitate. Her cries of '*sale bête*' are repeated by another Françoise, Zola's heroine, when her cow, hot for a neighbour's bull, drags her by the wrist through the meadows. Townspeople can still be appalled by the practicality, amounting to callousness, with which farmers regard their livestock: our neighbour, cornered by a crotchety *Charolais*, is known to express himself much more virulently than *la petite* Françoise. The farmer must always reckon with the resistance of what gives him his living. Before it yields, the earth, like the horse, has to be broken.

The French countryside is, traditionally, a menacing place; the towns from which today's tourists escape were built as refuges from its unpredictable hazards. Even today, when a villager's car is a more likely target for thieves than his domestic possessions, all our neighbours close and lock their shutters at night. The rural imagination was always full of bogeys, real and imagined: wolves and werewolves, taxmen and devils. In *Paris and its Provinces*, Richard Cobb recalls the justifiable apprehension with which travellers set out to pass through the king's forests. Bands of thieves (including one composed of notoriously audacious Jews) were ready to jump on any unprotected traveller. The country inn, and its restaurant, grew popular as sanctuaries where you might not leave unfleeced, but at least got something for your money. The tradition of rural hospitality remains warmly ambiguous: the size of the portions still to be found in unmodernized establishments, coupled with the insistence that the traveller eat all that is put before him, blends challenge with generosity.

In the fields of the Périgord, farmers still turn up the fangs of the sabre-toothed tiger whom their ancestors fought and venerated and whose blood, perhaps, is not wholly alien to them. Whoever assumes the geniality of the French countryside without respecting its atavistic strains and its antique origins runs the risk of being surprised by the uncertain temper both of its makers and of its seasons.

SPRING

The Cartesian prejudice of French thought gives abrupt definition to the seasons. In official theory, spring begins on 21 March, although along the Riviera – and even sometimes in the sheltered valley of the Dordogne – the mimosa forests will already have yellowed out in precocious flocculence. Certainly, the Niçois will have pelted each other with hot-house blooms in February's Battle of the Flowers long before any unforced symptoms of new life show themselves in our region.

In the South-West, the spring arrives with the hazing of the poplar crests. When the high branches begin to flare, they are at first less green than husky brown; their flittering flags signal the nascent season, even if the walnut trees (whose profitable fruit makes them pampered aristocrats) remain knuckled in wintery gauntness as their dead wood and unfruitful *gourmands* (suckers) are chain-sawed away in the last permitted trim before the sap rises. As for the poplars, their popularity derives from the tradition of planting a grove on the arrival of a female child, less in celebration than in order to be sure that she has a dowry: by the time she is of marriageable age, the quick timber will be ripe for sale.

A female child is not so much a blessing as a responsibility and, nearly always, a disappointment. Who will supply the muscles of the next generation? Immediately after our neighbour had produced yet another daughter, her mother-in-law looked in and observed, '*Fausse couche*': to produce a girl was no better than to miscarry. Where the future supplies neither promises nor pension, there is small pity. Fecundity (and the males it should entail) matters more in the country than fine opinions, though a wife must also know how to plant, drive a tractor and make *rillettes* and *boudin* and *confit* and preserve *foie gras* in the goose's own thick fat.

Late spring in the Forêt de Compiègne (left) near the village of
St-Jean-aux-Bois in the département of Oise.

The spring is still a season of wild flowers in the Dordogne. In our rumpled, widely forested department, the insecticides of the agro-business do not impose their colourless uniformity. The appearance of heavy-headed cowslips and the beady eyes of wild violets prompt domestic gardeners to consider putting their cloistered pots of geraniums out again in the open. Easter (when our neighbours will ask for a tribute of daffodils to dress the church) is the traditional time to believe that the new season is truly launched, though April and May can bring frosts curt enough to blast the gullible cherry trees, when – seduced by the March sun – their frail blossom offers hostages to climatic fortune.

Frosts strike with capricious venom in our hilly department; plums will escape while apricots are annihilated; fig-trees die back to the root, though they will 'push' (*pousse*) again almost at once and in five years pretty well regain their pristine abundance. In the Dordogne, such April cruelties are of marginal importance (as long as the belated walnut shoots are not scorched), but for the fruit-farmers of the neighbouring Lot and the Lot-et-Garonne, whose *pruneaux d'Agen* are an enrichingly famous crop, a sudden cold can be disastrous. Braziers and plastic mantles, hooped over the amenable blossom, guard against the consequences of those spring nights, unblanketed with cloud, when frost can strike like lightning from the clear sky.

In the wine-growing tracts of rural France – largely south of the jinking waistband of the Loire which divides our weather from that of the *nordistes* – the health of the vine determines whether the year will have a good or a notorious name. Each region, each *château* or bourgeois proprietor, trims and ties the stumpy source of his well-being in whatever manner tradition and his brand of grape demands. The appearance of the *vignobles* in the undulant and unpretentious Bergeracois is a shade less parade-ground rigid than it is in the flat, opulent Médoc, where the *grands crus* exact a standard of husbandry hardly to be distinguished from *haute coiffure*. Some *châteaux* prune their *pieds* almost to the ground, others leave leading stems attached to a high wire which, after a few months, will be braced with the green-freighted strain of the bulging crop.

There is an element of magic in viticulture; its precisions are both scientific and propitiatory: Dionysos/Bacchus is a god of mutable character and unchanging expectations. The first tribute to his new year comes in the form of 'Bordeaux mixture', that copper-sulphate prophylactic against the blighting mildew. Green-blue stains on vine-trellised farmhouse walls and shutters testify to the splashy diligence of the *patron*. The commercial vineyards use narrow-gauge tractors and fancy machines to spray their *appellation*-controlled hectares, but the peasant-farmer still totes his medicine on his back and pumps rhythmically as he doses his unnamed crop.

Last year's cuttings will have been bundled for kindling. They can also serve for grilling a succulent supper, as our old friend Martin Bamford, who presided over Château Loudenne, used to prove at his midsummer parties. The white ash gave a pungent heat with none of the unhealthy effects of the commercial char-coal which is bagged for the barbecues of camping *estivants*. In the economic conscience of the French peasant, nothing useful should be wasted; to be frugal is a kind of self-serving piety: gratitude and a certain parsimony go together.

Although his morals were less pious than his utterance, that old scoundrel Marshal Pétain did not gain the confidence of his compatriots by chance; despite being a *nordiste* (he was a native of the Pas de Calais), he had a shrewd sense of the mentality which informed *La France profonde* and which, although *grignotée* (nibbled away) by industrialization, still sustains the parochialism, the paranoia and the pride of the countryman. Pétain's reputation as a soldier was based on not asking too much of his men in the way of idle gestures; the peasants responded loyally, even credulously (look at the serried names on the war memorials in small country villages), to the Marshal's endorsement of their wary stoicism. The prin-ciple of *donnant-donnant*, which Pétain invoked so ingloriously in his dealings with the Nazis, was and remains part of the French peasant's way of life. In the Dordogne, which has few big farms and, unlike England, almost no rural working class, the tenant-farmer works his own land with the help only of his children and, perhaps, of his parents who may be too old for the fields but who will baby-sit, tend sheep and prepare *la soupe*, while the able-bodied are out at work. For the small-holder, the spring may involve more intensive work than a single family unit can manage in a brief time. *Donnant-donnant* then comes into season: farmers will lend each other days in order to complete whatever needs to be done in short order. No written record is kept, no money passes, but everyone knows the rogue who takes more than he gives, whether it is in planting the *tabac* (as key a crop here as the plum is in the Agenois) or humping the dry *foin* before a storm.

The first of May is a more reliable time to celebrate winter's end. The children of our region go on a ritual midnight rampage, demanding eggs from the farmers who, on this occasion at least, indulge their licensed pilfering. The official spring stretches to the June solstice, by which time the acacia has flowered whitely and *beignets* have been flavoured with its cloying savour. The lime-tree is being docked of its flowers (careful of the bees!), before they turn tastelessly brown, to be dried for digestive *infusions*. The bright days have stretched to their limit and been used, from dawn to dusk, while the long light is free and the heat is not too stifling. The spring months are both sweet and anxious; if they are too dry, the dreaded word *sécheresse* (drought) begins to be whispered, but if they are too well-watered, how is the *tabac* to be heeled into the mud, how will the vines escape the *mildiou*, no matter how often they are re-sprayed? What is good for one thing is bad for another. The printennial peasant can sometimes be cheerful, but he would be a fool to be complacent: there is still a long way to go to harvest-time.

Trees bordering a vineyard (above top) photographed in late April near the village of Roussillon in the département of Vaucluse.
(Below) Drifts of broom in late May colour the hillsides of the Montagne de l'Espérou near the summit of Mont Aigoual in the département of Gard.
(Overleaf) Winter still grips the landscape during the month of May on the hills above Champeix in the département of Puy-de-Dôme.

*April blossom covers the hillside terraces of the Montagne du Lubéron near the village
of Bonnieux in the département of Vaucluse.*

*Spring flowers border a tree-lined meadow (above) in the Marais Poitevin near the hamlet of le Vanneau in the département of Deux-Sèvres.
(Overleaf) Early spring in the Forêt de Lyons near the village of Lyons-la-Forêt in the département of Eure.*

*E*vening sunlight brightens the new spring foliage (left) of a poplar tree on a hillside
above the River Eyrieux near le Cheylard in the département of Ardèche.
(Above) Snow still clings to the Pyrenean peaks photographed in May from nearby the
hamlet of Cazenave in the département of Ariège.
(Overleaf) A fresh spring snowfall dusts the peaks of the Monts Dore in late May,
photographed from the hills near the hamlet of Vodable in the département
of Puy-de-Dôme.

The first vine shoots in May (left) lit by the setting sun in vineyards near the town of Pézenas in the département of Hérault.
(Above top) Late spring in vineyards near the wine village of Neffiès in the département of Hérault.
(Below) An early spring storm gathers over the vineyards and orchards that surround the Dentelles de Montmirail in the département of Vaucluse.
(Overleaf) Wild daffodils blooming at the beginning of June in a meadow near the village of Egliseneuve-d'Entraigues in the département of Puy-de-Dôme.

*A waterfall in the Cirque de Baume photographed in early spring near the village of
Baumes-les-Messieurs in the département of Jura.*

Late spring in the upper valley of the Loire (above) near the village of Arlempdes in the département of Haute-Loire.
(Overleaf) Storm clouds over the landscape of the Auvergne photographed in April near the Puy d'Ysson in the département of Puy-de-Dôme.

*Spring foliage emerging (left) on the mountainsides surrounding the village of St-Béat
in the département of Haute-Garonne.
(Above top) May blossom along the Route des Corniches above the valley of the Ariège
near les Cabannes in the département of Ariège.
(Below) The upper valley of the River Tarn photographed on an early May evening
near the village of Pont-de-Montvert in the département of Lozère.
(Overleaf) A willow blooms in May near the village of Olloix above the valley of the
Couze de Chambon in the département of Puy-de-Dôme.*

Early spring in the country lanes near St-Rémy-de-Provence in the département of Bouches-du-Rhône.

*A May storm brewing (above top) in the mountains above the Vallée de Chaudefour near the Puy de Sancy in the département of Puy-de-Dôme.
(Below) Judas trees in full bloom, photographed in late April in the Massif de la Ste Baume in the département of Var.
(Overleaf) A misty April morning on the River Loir near the village of Luché-Pringé in the département of Sarthe.*

An early crop of rape flowering in May on the farmland of the Orvin valley near the village of Marcilly-le-Hayer in the département of Aube.

*Spring lambs grazing in the valley of the Viaur near Réquista
in the département of Aveyron.*

SUMMER

There are no certainties in our region. By the end of June, when summer is official, we can already have had a *canicule* scorching enough to turn the Dordogne into a rivulet dribbling listlessly between bushy islands which, in another year, scarcely froth the rush of the weltering waters. Primed with the spent snows of the Auvergne and the Corrèze and gorged with the storms that drown the young corn and bog the tractors, the Dordogne can then gush with menace before subsiding to please the soft canoeists.

Hail is a regular summer hazard. Its symptoms are heavy grey-black clouds with a nervous white trim. The size of the hailstones is a subject of awful rumour: they are sometimes said to be as big as pigeons' eggs, sometimes bigger than your fist. I was promised only last year that one district was pelted with *rectangular* hail – slabs of ice that dented cars and slashed vines to leafy ribbons, putting an end to vintage hopes. Even the modest buckshot which pelts most commonly from unreliable summer skies poxes the green jackets of the young walnuts, giving ruinous access to the worms which insinuate themselves in the embryonic flesh. Heavy falls can flatten the ripening corn as if some malevolent and gigantic cat had rolled in it. We used often to hear the boom of rockets when hail was announced, although this method of puncturing the clouds – so that they dumped their loads on a neighbour rather than on the owner of the artillery – seems now less popular. Perhaps it led to too much violent or litigious recrimination; perhaps it was simply too expensive and ineffective to be worth the trouble.

If the spring has been hot, the hotels and camping grounds along the rivers will already be full. The misfortune of some, the French often say, makes for the well-being of others: hoteliers rejoice in conditions which cause peasants to shake

Poppies colour a neglected meadow (left) near the village of St-Maur in the département of Cher.

their heads. The symbiosis of tourism and agriculture is far from perfect: each has different hopes and expectations from the same climate. The peasant is essential to the beauty on which the hotelier and the tour operator depend, but the tourist contributes little to the well-being of the farmer on whose land he is happy to wander. The *ferme-auberge*, where visitors can taste the true fruits of the region in homely circumstances, is the countryman's attempt to make tourism yet another crop.

Nowadays, of course, one does not call a peasant a peasant (certainly not to his face); they are all *agriculteurs*, a cant denomination intended to emancipate them from metropolitan condescensions. However, what they do not like to be called by others is certainly what they are still proud to consider themselves. Their complexions, their dress and their habits mark them out; their face and posture are functions of the landscape and the seasons: that tan is the wind, those lines are the sun. The man is worked by the land he works.

The *agriculteur*'s trade is dangerous as well as interminable. A few summers ago, the farmer on the far side of our valley, with whom I played in a football match one August day when it was too hot for a wise man to roll a *boule*, was chewed to death, in front of his son, when the corner of his cardigan was caught in the threshing machine. The son works on, alone with his mother, but he has not smiled since that fatal day. Death always lived in Arcadia, as the old proverb promised; it needs only a moment of negligence or bad luck to bring it home to us. After such a sudden tragedy, the neighbours and *cousins* converge on the bereaved household with instinctive solidarity. Our condolences may be accepted but we are made aware that we can never truly belong to peasant society or share its battles.

Until recently, the local *patois* was the secret language of those who truly belonged to the region; his incomprehension excluded the stranger better than any locked gate. Unfortunately, *occitan* is now an endangered species of speech confined mostly to the grand-parental generation. Sound too colours a landscape and the decline of *patois*, with its furtive humours, is a symptom of the growing monotony, that homogenization of Europe which the farmers, at once petty and noble, see as the rupture of a long tradition. The banalities of television and the neo-Jacobinism of Brussels threaten a particularism which has taken millennia to grow.

In his elegy for the Périgord which he entitled *The Generous Earth*, Philip Oyler wrote an account, more obituary than he knew, of life in our region before the tourist and the motor car. Himself a farmer, Oyler conceded mastery to the old Périgourdin whose grateful frugality wasted nothing, least of all the droppings of his animals, which were hoarded to supplement the strength of soil which has been exploited by man for longer, perhaps, than any other part of Europe.

When we first lived in the Périgord, *le père* Barat often brought his horse to crop the field in which, *en bons bourgeois*, we later put our swimming pool (the rock had to be blasted with dynamite before the alien breach could be plumbed), but his son has two tractors now, and no horses. The old man used to come down and stand in 'our' land, on summer evenings, quite as if the title had never passed to us from the improvident villager who sold it. It was not that old Barat resented our living on his hill – houses are less significant to the peasant than the land which surrounds them – but that our presence, which he welcomed *socially*, with a polite sweep of his cap, was incompatible with any practical activity that he could recognize as worthwhile.

Although the horse is now either a rarity or a chic pastime, summer visitors can find our side roads entirely blocked by two Périgourdins who – meeting from opposite directions – have stopped their cars and lean across to talk to each other, like horsemen who have reined in under the thick shake of a chestnut tree. Hooted by aliens, they will finish their sentences, or their paragraphs, and proceed at no more than the equivalent of a fast walk, measuring the husky height and complexion of the maize or the wheat as they move unabashedly on. No country-man will hasten his business, whether at a garage or in a shop, because someone else is waiting; the virtue of impatience has no claim on him.

It is not only the means of labour which have changed in the French countryside. In the great plains of the Somme and the Beauce, mechanization has gone so far that you might as well be in the Ukraine or the Middle West of America, but even in the south-west there are new crops and methods. Our neigh-bours' main source of revenue is tobacco, a state monopoly whose guaranteed price was always a bankable hedge against fickle circumstance, but that sweet-smelling, fast-growing, labour-intensive staple is losing its reliable allure: despite its vested interest, the French government has recognized the perniciousness of the once ubiquitous Gaulloise. Summer fields are still fleshy with the inedible lushness of tobacco plants, but mop-headed hectares of sun-flowers are beginning to make themselves at home. The saleable seed secretes light, digestible oil which, when it comes to salads, the Périgourdin prefers to enrich with glutinous walnut oil. More and more fields now take on the colour of madness as the summer sun prompts early green to Van Goghian yellow. If the heat is too fierce and too pro-longed, the lolling heads die down and the yellow blackens into premature desicca-tion, with sorry consequences for the peasant's balance sheet, even though the high season's holiday-makers find nothing but pleasure in the long hot landscape.

*Buttercups and poplar trees photographed at the end of May near the hamlet of
Arcais in the département of Deux-Sèvres.
(Overleaf) A midsummer landscape in the gorges of the River Verdon in the département of
Alpes-de-Haute-Provence.*

*June flowers cover the clifftops at the Pointe de Minard to the north-west of St-Brieuc
in the département of Côtes-du-Nord.*

*The coastline of the Cotentin photographed in midsummer near the lighthouse
at Cap Lévy in the département of Manche.
(Overleaf) Hazy July sunshine lights the River Ouysse near le Moulin de Cougnaguet
to the west of Rocamadour in the département of Lot.*

A field of sunflowers (left) in early August near the village of Châtillon-en-Diois in the département of Drôme. (Above top) Summer wildflowers colour the hedgerows in the hills to the south-west of Charolles in the département of Saône-et-Loire. (Below) A carpet of heather blooms on the heathland of the Sologne, photographed at the end of August near Chaumont-sur-Tharonne in the département of Loir-et-Cher. (Overleaf) A summer meadow in the Marais Poitevin near the riverside village of Coulon in the département of Deux-Sèvres.

A field of lavender (left) in full bloom photographed at the end of July near the village of Ferrassières in the département of Drôme. (Above top) A lone tree set in a field of flowering rape near Mur-de-Bretagne in the département of Côtes-du-Nord. (Below) A walnut tree in a ripening field of rye in the valley of the River Oule, near the village of la Charce, in the département of Drôme. (Overleaf) A screen of trees, planted to protect the Provençal orchards from the Mistral, near the village of Eygalières in the département of Bouches-du-Rhône.

In early July, summer at last reaches the upper valley of the River Ouzon near the village of Arbéost in the département *of* Hautes-Pyrénées.

*Early summer in the valley of the River Orb (above) near the village of Roquebrun in
the département of Hérault.
(Overleaf) The coastline of Cap Fréhel photographed in early summer near
Sables-d'Or-les-Pins in the département of Côtes-du-Nord.*

*A field of lavender photographed at the end of July near Forcalquier
in the* département *of Alpes-de-Haute-Provence.*

*A crop of flax flowering in June (above) in the Pays de Bray near the village of
Fouarmont in the département of Seine-Maritime.
(Overleaf) A cloud of smoke from a summer forest fire in the Montagne du Lubéron shadows a
ripe cornfield near the village of Jouques in the département of Vaucluse.*

*High summer in the Massif de l'Esterel near the Pic de l'Ours
in the département of Var.*

*S*ummer pastures in the Hourquette d'Ancizan (above) near Arreau in the
département of Hautes-Pyrénées.
(Overleaf) A midsummer sunset over the bay of Morlaix in the
département of Finistère.

AUTUMN

The late-blooming flags of the *soir d'été* (Lagerstroemia), pink, red and purple, announce the surrender of summer to autumn, although there is often small sign of appeasement in the weather. August can be the hottest month, when anxious farmers pump water to their radiant sprinklers to keep crops unscorched (maize rattles ominously in the dry winds); wine-growers hope for a happy balance between sugar-generating warmth and the moisture needed to plump the ripening grapes. September is still green, although the calendar decrees, on the 21st, that autumn is here. The conclusive caesura comes as the camping sites and the hotels lose their customers and the canoeists quit the rivers.

The *rentrée*, when the schools again open their doors and the *grandes vacances* end, is the hinge of the French year. It used to be that almost all French families headed for the sea in August. When the 1936 Popular Front introduced paid holidays (a move regarded as virtual Bolshevism by the bourgeoisie), the *glissement vers le soleil* presaged today's avalanche, to which Germans, Dutch, Scandinavians and the British add their pale weight. The back-up from the Mediterranean has lent glamour to the *monde rural*; few Parisian holiday-makers gave more than a literally passing thought to the countryside in the days before the Riviera was lined with caravans and its seas soured with pollution. After Jean-Paul Sartre's comfortable cousins were evacuated from Alsace to the Périgord in the autumn of 1939, they reported with horror on the habits of the savages with whom they were obliged to consort. The smoke-blackened houses and crusty complexion of the natives belonged to a world utterly alien to their own.

Late autumn colours (left) tinge the trees in the Massif de la Chartreuse near the village of Entremont-le-Vieux in the département of Savoie.

If the Périgourdin peasant is now rarely dependent for warmth only on his own fireplace (or on its *crémaillère* to heat his *pot au feu*), his woods are still prudently re-planted. Casual timber is stored for domestic purposes, but the lanes are ramparted with corded lumber, identically measured for commercial use. The chestnut is for floors; furniture and *charpenterie* use the oak, whose roots have fostered the fabled and costly truffle (now hunted not with the traditional sniffy pig but with a variant of the metal detector). The wood-workers of the Périgord form an exclusive and prosperous guild; our village *menuisier* has five houses which he rents to summer people, all paid for by a skill which was learnt from an illiterate master who taught him not only to make shutters, windows and doors but also to match the panelling and furniture styles of all the relevant Louis, from XI to XV.

The *arrière-saison* can be the sweetest of the year, although its heat is not as high nor its pleasures as languid as those of August. The *rentrée* is a time when politicians unroll their shirt-sleeves, after their summer *assises*, and resume their Parisian suits and phrases. Many of the deputies are also mayors of their own towns and villages, and even the grandest of them will be sure to keep his roots as earthy as he can: President Mitterrand keeps an annual hiking tryst with the landscape and the people of the Morbihan, where he was a *maquisard* in the Resistance whose brave, if exaggerated, mythology comforts the bruised vanity of the French. *Maquis* is the name given to the scrub in which partisans have always found it easy to operate; thus the landscape itself supplies the name and the opportunity which enabled some Frenchmen to save their country's honour. René Char, a Provençal poet who wrote of a changeable autumn going 'more quickly back and forth than a gardener's rake', was among the first.

Memories of the countryside in which they found it impossible to make a living sustain innumerable citizens whom the casual visitor would assume to be Parisians. It is said that the majority of taxi-drivers in the capital come from the Auvergne; there was, until recently, a Paris newspaper printed exclusively for Auvergnat exiles. A Paris taxi-driver, learning where I had come from, told me that he still owned a plot of land near Domme where he intended to build a place for his retirement. Meanwhile, he would repair there sometimes simply for the pleasure of sitting in his own *pays*. In every Parisian traffic-jam there are men dreaming of an *arrière-saison* south of the Loire, where summer's lease can last at least until Toussaint and we have had roses bloom for the fourth time in one year.

The first weeks of autumn are especially busy for our neighbours. The *remorque* is towed up and down the hill ceaselessly, with Rémy and Gaëtan installed on the top of the bales. They have to duck under the branches of our lime-tree whose nervous leaves are now crisp from months of sun. The white grapes have lost their acidity as the sugar pearls their flesh. Pickers beware of the gorging hornets who will later come banging on the lighted windows. The dark grapes are as purple now as a vintner's prose. Anxious eyes measure the walnuts as they drop their first inedible samples; the cash crop will not fall till the first rains loosen their moorings and the wind brings them down. Meanwhile, we want enough showers to help them put on weight. Brown fingers are the symptom of autumn in walnut country (lemon juice is the antidote).

Our neighbours are worrying about the tobacco: if it has escaped the hail, and been watered enough to bring it to first-grade maturity, the heavy stems of now paling green leaves still have to be cut, carted and hung in the *séchoir*, which will almost certainly have to be heated so that the leaves are ready for sorting and grading, by hand, before the end of November. On sullen afternoons, the barns steam like overworked horses.

As for the grape harvest, the timing of the *vendange* is determined by a mixture of instinct and probabilities. To pick too early is to miss the chance of a more succulent and juicier crop; to leave it to mid-October could incur disastrous storms. In the unassuming vineyards of the Périgord, the *vendange* is a backbreaking outing in which the whole neighbourhood is involved. Part of the ritual consists in all the pickers being invited to eat a bunch of grapes at the same time, after which one spits out the seeds in an unconscious echo of the apotropaic gesture – *po, po, po* – beloved of the Greeks. Is this done to replenish the earth or in appeasement of Bacchus, whose substance is being consumed? No peasant can furnish the reason any more than he will forgo the practice.

The Périgourdin no longer adds his wine to his soup as his ancestors did, before lifting the dish to their lips, but he retains a keen palate and, very often, a private *barrique* where he ferments his own *petits vins*. Our neighbour's cellar has a vast barrel to whose bubblesome fermentation he invites you to listen as if to the trailer of a forthcoming attraction. The peasants, to their chagrin, no longer have the right to distil their own *liqueurs*, although the *eaux de vie* of our region, usually walnut or pear-flavoured, are famous for purity and power. A good helping of marinated *pruneaux d'Agen* is, they say, better than a 'flu shot and certainly more painless.

There was such a fuss, soon after the war, when the government proposed to dock the country people of their right to make their own *liqueurs* (on account of the revenue Paris lost on unlicensed stills), that a compromise was agreed, allowing those who already possessed the right to retain it, with a ten-litre limit, although their heirs would not. Perhaps in consequence, there was a cult of longevity; even now, there are enough old gentlemen to give regular autumnal employment to the distiller who comes, with his marvellously intricate machinery – burnished copper belly and shiny tripes, belt-driven energy and metal wheels like an engine of war – to give them their due. It is no scandalous secret that the ten-litre limit is not always observed to the last decimal place ('*Après tout, monsieur, nous ne sommes pas des Suisses!*'). Supplied with a glass, the distiller can be persuaded to a certain liberality. It is, after all, in nobody's interest, except the taxman's, that the industrially produced stuff, with its petro-chemical nose, should take the place of what is truly worth drinking. '*L'alcool*,' said Brillat-Savarin, '*est le monarque des liquides.*' Certainly, it is the only king a peasant bows to.

The *arrière-saison* may begin with days indistinguishable from summer, but by Toussaint, on the cusp of October and November, when the pots of chrysanthemums are massed in the market for the *Fête des Morts*, the landscape will have gone through its implacable variations of costume on the way to winter's minimalism. Luckily, the forests are not quick-change artists; the golds and reds linger as the days shorten. Further south, the *Tramontane* and the *Mistral* unclothe the landscape with less ceremony, but the Périgord strips languidly, leaving huddles of royal colour beneath the thinning branches. The claret remnants of the *vendange* lie in heaps of wrung-out lees to flavour the air with musty promises.

After Toussaint, the countryman resigns himself to rain. If it has come late, he can be seen scuffing in his boots in the bald patches of ground under his walnut trees for the last blackening falls. November is the time for killing the ducks who have gorged themselves on summer's plenty and are consigned, with the mercilessness of routine, to fill the tins and jars to delight next year's crop of tourists. It is not only the masters of fashion who must ready themselves for summer as winter comes in. *'Tout passe,'* said Théophile Gautier. Echoing the last words of Sartre's *Huis Clos,* the peasant murmurs, *'Recommençons'*. Already the buds are glistening on the cherry-trees.

Late October in the valley of the Isère near the village of St-Pierre-d'Albigny in the département of Savoie.

*A late September storm (above) brewing over the Monts Dore near the village of
Besse-en-Chandesse in the département of Puy-de-Dôme.
(Overleaf) A damp, misty autumn morning in the Forêt de Compiègne near
Pierrefonds in the département of Oise.*

*An autumnal poplar tree photographed in October near Corneilla-de-Conflent at the
foot of the Massif du Canigou in the département of Pyrénées-Orientales.*

A peach orchard (above top) in the valley of the River Têt photographed in October
near the village of Eus in the département of Pyrénées-Orientales.
(Below) A lone fig tree takes on its autumn colour in the vineyards of the Massif des
Maures near the village of Plan-de-la-Tour in the département of Var.
(Overleaf) A field of sunflowers photographed in late September near the village of
Flamarens in the département of Gers.

Late autumn in the Forêt de Compiègne (left) near the village of St Jean-aux-Bois in the département of Oise.
(Above top) Fallen autumn leaves in the Forêt de Compiègne in the département of Oise.
(Below) An autumnal creeper covers a derelict barn in the hamlet of Cressin in the département of Ain.
(Overleaf) Late autumn in the valley of the Isère photographed from nearby the village of Miolans in the département of Savoie.

*A misty autumn morning (left) in the Fôret de Lyons near the village of
Lyons-la-Forêt in the département of Eure.
(Above top) Cherry trees and grape vines photographed in late autumn near the village
of Irancy in the département of Yonne.
(Below) Heather flowering in October under the pine trees of les Landes, photographed
near the village of Sabres in the département of Landes.
(Overleaf) An early autumn evening in the Gave des Cauterets near
Pierrefitte-Nestalas in the département of Hautes-Pyrénées.*

*A Gascon landscape photographed in October near Condom
in the département of Gers.*

*A field of sunflowers (above) photographed at the end of September near the village of
Marcilly-le-Hayer in the département of Aube.
(Overleaf) The valley of the Isère photographed in late October from the Col du Granier
in the département of Savoie.*

*Autumnal trees in the Forêt de Compiègne near the village of
Pierrefonds in the département of Oise.*

A late autumn evening (above) in the Massif des Monédières near the village of
Chaumeil in the département of Corrèze.
(Overleaf) Champagne vineyards photographed in early November on the Côtes des Blancs
near the village of Grauves in the département of Marne.

*An early autumn view of the high Alps photographed near the village of
Mont-Saxonnex in the département of Haute-Savoie.*

*L*ate autumn in the mountains (above) near the village of Montségur in the
département *of Ariège.*
*(Overleaf) The Montagne de Reims photographed on a late autumn evening
near the village of Bouzy in the département of Marne.*

*A field of millet photographed in late September near the village of
St-Clar in the département of Gers.*

Fields of grain harvested and ploughed at the end of September near Issoire in the département of Puy-de-Dôme.

WINTER

'Hiver', said Charles d'Orléans in the fifteenth century, 'vous n'êtes qu'un vilain!' Winter's villainy is less monstrous in our region than it is further north or to the east: the mountains of the Massif Central, up towards the Puy de Dôme, are scarfed with white almost every year, as its modest winter sporting facilities announce. In the Savoie, of course, there is no modesty: the mountains are the living of the people and winter brings their happiest harvest. Good snow is as precious à la montagne as a good vintage in the Bordelais.

The Périgord rarely undergoes violent falls in temperature, although we have known it to be minus twenty centigrade, the eaves daggered with icicles and the fish-pond as solidly marbled as a tombstone. The usual mildness is not always a blessing; if we can have sunbathing days in February, a lack of frosts keeps pests alive. The peasant will always find a reason to shake his head: too little rain fails to fill the sous-couches and entails next year's drought; too much makes ploughing impossible, drowns the winter wheat and, in very bad years, clogs the meadows in the valleys. The cold may scorch our neighbour's cheeks as he goes out, huddled in his work-clothes which the wind swells into gargantuan forms, but the earth is more rewarding to work if the clods have been crisped by the frost of at least a few clear nights. The mornings then glitter with the beady confectionery of spiders' webs hammocked between the wayside weeds.

France is always said, and with reason, to be divided in two, politically and geographically. I confess that we have spent negligible amounts of time in the flat north and none in the pine-grim forests of Alsace, where the goose is cultivated as ruthlessly as it is in the Périgord. If January is less rude here, it is a time for indoor work, when the peasant's wife fills her kitchen with the basins and tubs in

An early winter's snowfall (left) dusts the trees beside the Lac Noir on the Route des Crêtes in the département of Haut-Rhin.

which almost every part of the recently slaughtered pig has its distinct recipe. The reek of death is slowly mollified into the perhaps disgraceful prospect of gastronomic pleasure. Brillat-Savarin suggested that there was greater conjugal joy in a shared table than in a shared bed. Is it a slander to say that the Périgord is more famous for its cooks than for their beauty? Winter is the season of their contentment, when bottling and canning (a routine artisanal habit) give exemption from outdoor tasks. Mallarmé spoke of *'l'hiver, saison de l'art serein'*; though I am not sure that he had gastronomy in mind, he might as well have been referring to the almost instinctive competence of unstarred chefs in the smoke-crusted kitchens of rural France.

While the women turn to their pots, observing the almost unchanged role of the female in the *monde rural*, the men – no longer obliged to be gatherers – put on mottled khaki and become hunters again. The annual war against the rabbit is also, in its season, a pitiless, ritualistic assault on the hare and the deer and the *sanglier*, whose hirsute tuskiness is also emblematic of the region. Like his Cro-Magnon ancestor, the Périgourdin is both the enemy and the familiar of the game he tracks or, more often, lies in wait for. Certain species have been hunted almost to extinction and are now, supposedly, protected. Among them are the *fouines* (martens), whose bushy beauty cannot disguise their savagery.

The *fouine* is a vicious predator, the terror of the chicken coop and an alarming squatter in any farmhouse roof which admits his slinky entrance into a warm *grenier* (hay loft). Eager to pass the cold weeks in parasitic tenancy, *fouines* have none of the tact of the mouse or the rat, who tends to observe neighbourly hours and who returns home with no heavy tread. The use of fibre glass to insulate our tiled roofs furnishes the marten with ripping material for his nest. Once ensconced, *fouines* are almost impossible to evict. You are sold *bombes* whose smoke, once the touch-paper is lit, is said to serve permanent notice to quit, but it is less easy to be sure that it has permeated the necessary niches. We did not solve our problem, despite the discreet use of clever traps, which caught the beautiful creatures alive (after which Monsieur is free to deal with them as he sees fit, as long as the *garde champêtre* does not catch him at it), until we removed and relaid our entire roof, sealing the previously permissive access-points with exclusive concrete. We listen to the winter silence with unmitigated relief.

Winter strips the anatomy of the landscape and lays bare its fundamental economy. Now we recognize the importance of the summer's unapplauded rituals of hedging and ditching. In our hilly department, where the higher slopes are often so steep that the rains have washed them bald, good drainage is essential. Many of our older buildings are stilted above what, in summer, seem to be unthreatening valley sites. At Périgueux, just below the cathedral, there is a particularly lovely instance of a medieval barn, crutched with upholding beams which spread out from a single narrow stone 'keel' and keep its 'cargo' immune from any conceivable rise of the River Isle.

The paradox of our official winter is that it *begins* with the shortest day of the year. But the world of the peasant is not truly amenable to Cartesian definitions, nor is Christmas always his main winter festival: the Latin countries tend to give presents on twelfth night, which the Christian fathers wisely appropriated to their calendar, although it almost certainly owes its magic to earlier beliefs. In his study of the carnival at Romans, in the Drôme, which was most famous in the sixteenth century, Emmanuel Le Roy Ladurie gives us good reason to remember that Rabelais, not Descartes, is the true philosopher of *la France profonde*. The midwinter revels in Romans offer a gorgeously menacing instance of the peasants' capacity for inventive duplicities, for the interplay of enmity and friendship, the wooing of nature and its mockery, the teasing of scapegoats and the coronation of scoundrels. The gentry expected to be satirized and was expected to smile, during this rural Saturnalia, at the groundlings' promises to make cuckolds of them all.

The winter *fête* at Romans (and elsewhere) took place in February, when people could begin to hope that winter was beginning to abate its rigidity. The appearance of friend bear, if he emerged from hibernation, became a happy augury. He would look at the sky and, if it were cloudy, he stayed awake; clear skies implied more frosts, which led him to close his eyes again. Yet the amiable bear was also, in the Pyrenees, the sheep-stealer whose carnival impersonator the peasants would shoot, in symbolic form, while admiring his sexual insolence (he was licensed to grope the females just as he pillaged the honeycombs).

I once happened to arrive at night in a village near Carcassonne on Mardi

Gras and was amazed, and a little scared, at the vigour with which the crowd attacked each other, and strangers, with papier-mâché phalli, whose symbolic place in the rites of spring – which was imminent – needed no anthropologist to disclose. This playfulness has been known to get savagely out of hand; the most notorious case was a midsummer fair in 1870, in the north of our department, near Nontron, which led to a horrifying murder. The strong-stomached can find a full and fascinating account of it, and of the realities of country life in nineteenth-century Arcadia, in Alain Corbin's 'The Village of Cannibals'.

Winter may be a villain and, as Jean Richepin called it, *'tueur des pauvres gens'*, but its villainies are sexual as well as murderous: it is in January and February, after all, that spring's lambs and autumn's babies are made. Hibernation is a time of renewal; frost makes men and beasts seek each other's heat. The seasons are never simple, never discrete; they bleed into and mimic each other. Winter kills, but *'si le grain ne meurt'*, how can it come springing to life?

Bare-branched trees (above) photographed in January on the mountain slopes below Puy Mary in the département of Cantal.
(Overleaf) The setting sun lights the distinctive shape of Mont Granier, photographed on a late February evening from the village of Entremont-le-Vieux in the département of Savoie.

*A fall of snow at the beginning of winter on the Col de Valouse in the
département of Drôme.*

A plantation of poplars (above) photographed in February near
Champagne-en-Valromy in the département of Ain.
(Overleaf) The River Ibie photographed in late winter near the village of
les Salelles in the département of Ardèche.

*A newly ploughed field photographed on a cold, frosty morning in February near
Nitry in the département of Yonne.*

A February hoar-frost (above) coats the landscape near the village of Azincourt in the département of Pas-de-Calais.
(Overleaf) A late January evening in the Canche valley near the village of Beaurainville in the département of Pas-de-Calais.

*E*arly winter storm clouds (left) gather over Mont Granier, photographed from
the village of St Pierre-de-Soucy in the département of Savoie.
(Above top) The vineyards of the Chautagne photographed after a February sunset
near the village of Ruffieux in the département of Savoie.
(Below) The Ternoise valley photographed on a frosty February morning near the
village of Blangy-sur-Ternoise in the département of Pas-de-Calais.
(Overleaf) A January sunset over the Dentelles de Montmirail, photographed near the
hamlet of Suzette in the département of Vaucluse.

A winter waterfall in the Vallée de Chaudefour near le Mont-Dore in the département of Puy-de-Dôme.

*The vineyards of the Côtes de Beaune (above) photographed in January near the
village of Pommard in the département of Côte-d'Or.
(Overleaf) The Ternoise valley photographed in February near the village of
Tilly-Capelle in the département of Pas-de-Calais.*

The frozen Cascade de l'Eventail in the valley of the Hérisson photographed in February near the village of Bonlieu in the département of Jura.

A February landscape (above top) in the Vercors photographed near the village of St-Julien-en-Vercors in the département of Drôme.
(Below) The Col de Rousset photographed in late winter near the summit above the town of Die in the département of Drôme.
(Overleaf) The Entremont valley in the Massif de la Chartreuse photographed in January from the village of Entremont-le-Vieux in the département of Savoie.

A newly ploughed field in the Créquoise valley (left) photographed in February near the hamlet of Lebiez in the département of Pas-de-Calais.
(Above top) A February sunset in the Authie valley near the hamlet of Douriez in the département of Pas-de-Calais.
(Below) A late winter's afternoon on the mountain slopes of Puy Mary near the village of Mandailles in the département of Cantal.
(Overleaf) The valley of the River Isère photographed in February from the Col du Granier in the département of Savoie.

A late winter's evening on the hills above the Loue valley near
Ornans in the département of Doubs.